PUPPETS & COSTUMES

By Sidney Martin and Dana McMillan
Illustrated by Corbin Hillam

Publisher: Roberta Suid
Editor: Elizabeth Russell
Cover Design: David Hale
Design and Production: Susan Pinkerton
Cover Art: Corbin Hillam

Monday Morning is a registered trademark
of Monday Morning Books, Inc.

Entire contents copyright © 1986 by Monday Morning
Books, Inc., Box 1680, Palo Alto, California 94302

ISBN 0-912107-45-6

Printed in the United States of America

9 8 7 6 5 4 3 2

Contents

Introduction   4

Puppets   5
Paper Bag Puppet   6
Envelope Puppet   7
Marionette   8
Paper Plate Puppet   9
Head Puppet   10
Trash Bag Puppet   11
Foam Rubber Puppet   12
Tongue Depressor Puppet   13
Mini Puppet Stage   14
Pop-Up Puppet   15
Body Puppet   16
Caterpillar Rod Puppet   17
Jumping Jack Puppet   18
Mop Puppet   20
Folded Puppet   21
Milk Carton Puppet   22
Maxi Puppet Stage   23
City Building   24

Costumes   25
Basic Pillow Case Costume   26
    Clown, Flapper, Lizard, Baseball Player,
    Coat and Tails
Basic Paper Costume   34
    Scarecrow, Indian Shirt, Brown Bear, Bee,
    Knight, Lion, Fairy Princess, Bat
Basic Fabric Costume   46
    Mouse, Skunk, Carrot

Masks and Props   51
Primitive Mask   52
Funny Eyeglasses   53
Vinyl Mask   54
Visor Cap   56
Insect Mask   58

Musical Instruments   59
Pie Tin Tambourine   60
Rattler   61
Finger Cymbals   62
Sand Blocks   63
Bottle Chimes   64

Introduction

The projects in *Puppets and Costumes* are easy to make. They don't require a sewing maching or artistic talent. Instead, they have time-saving directions and use inexpensive materials and craft supplies such as scissors, glue, and markers. Fastening is done with glue, tape, staples, or laces.

The joy of creating puppets and costumes need not be limited to Halloween or an annual play. Teachers, parents, students, and youth group leaders will find many ways to use the ideas in this book. A puppet or costume can make a story come alive for children working on language development. Even for the simplest stage show or play, a costume makes the experience that much more rewarding.

These activities were developed by The Learning Exchange, a nonprofit educational resource center which helps school districts improve quality of education. Hundreds of people have returned to The Learning Exchange each year to participate in our costuming and puppet workshops. Part of the excitement of these workshops is the opportunity to create a personalized version of the many projects on display. Please use imagination and experiment freely with these ideas. The puppet or costume may change during the making, perhaps turning out much different from our suggestion. That's okay!

Here are some suggested materials and sources. Any simliar material can usually be substituted.

Pillowcases . . . . hospital or linen supply
Trash bags . . . . grocery or hardware store
Self-adhesive paper . . . . drug, hardware, variety stores
Paper plates . . . . grocery store
Yarn . . . . craft supply or variety store
Cardboard . . . . packing boxes
Vinyl scraps . . . . auto upholstery shop
Fur remnants . . . . coat factory

Sidney Martin and
Dana McMillan
The Learning Exchange, Inc.
2720 Walnut
Kansas City, MO 64111

PUPPETS

Paper Bag Puppet

Create a wise, old owl or anything you can imagine.

MATERIALS:
Paper lunch bag
Orange felt scrap
2 brown beans
White glue
Colored markers
Brown feathers (optional)

CONSTRUCTION:
1. Cut a piece of construction paper to fit the side of the paper bag and another piece to fit the bottom. Glue the paper to the bag.
2. Draw feathers on the body as shown or glue on real feathers.
3. Cut two triangular beaks from orange felt and glue on the face.
4. Glue on the two beans for eyes.

USE:
Place hand in the bag with fingers around the natural fold. Move fingers to open and close the puppet's mouth.

Envelope Puppet

Use smaller envelopes for smaller hands.

MATERIALS:
2 envelopes of identical size
2 paper loops (about 1″ diameter)
Scraps of construction paper, felt, yarn
White glue

CONSTRUCTION:
1. Fold each envelope in half crosswise, then fold back the other way to form a crease.
2. Slip one envelope inside the other with glued edges of flaps facing each other.
3. Bend the envelopes along the crease so that the two lower corners come together.
4. Glue a paper loop on each side of the center fold inside the envelopes.
5. Cut features from scraps to create a chicken, an owl, or any other creature. Glue them on and allow glue to dry thoroughly.

USE:
Place hand in the envelope puppet. Put middle finger in the upper loop and thumb in the lower loop. The loops allow a better grasp to open and close the mouth.

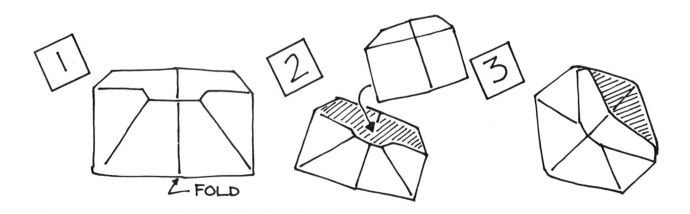

Marionette

Walk this puppet around as you talk for him.

MATERIALS:
12" x 18" posterboard
Rubber cement
Four 3" x 30" strips of construction paper
2" x 12" cardboard strip
Heavyweight paper
Colored markers
Yarn
Construction paper or wallpaper
Hole punch

CONSTRUCTION:
1. Fold the posterboard in half crosswise. Fold each half in half again toward the center crease. Overlap the two end flaps to form a triangular tube. Glue the end flaps together.
2. Cut a head with a long neck from heavyweight paper. Draw on a face with markers and glue on yarn hair.
3. Glue the neck to the back inside of the body.
4. Pleat the four strips and glue onto the body as arms and legs.
5. Cut hands and feet from construction paper and glue onto the arms and legs.
6. Glue or staple the hands to the ends of the cardboard strip. Punch a hole in the center of the strip and another in the top of the head. Loop a piece of yarn through the holes and tie the ends together.

USE:
Tilt the cardboard strip in various directions to move the arms and legs.

Paper Plate Puppet

This puppet might be named Mr. Big Mouth.

MATERIALS:
3 paper plates
Scraps of fabric, felt, colored paper, yarn, styrofoam
Glue
Stapler
Colored markers

CONSTRUCTION:
1. Design the features for the top of the head. Cut out of scraps and staple or glue them to a paper plate.
2. Color another plate pink or red with a marker. Fold this plate in half to form the mouth.
3. Staple the top and bottom plates to the mouth at the edges, leaving the back open.

USE:
Put hand in the back opening. Place thumb below the folded inner plate and fingers above it. Move thumb and fingers to open and close the mouth.

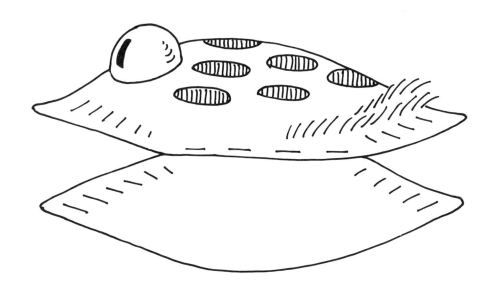

Head Puppet

Wear this puppet for a play.

MATERIALS:
Large grocery bag
Scraps of colored paper, felt, fabric, buttons, yarn
Glue
Colored markers

CONSTRUCTION:
1. Fold two inches of the open end of the bag toward the inside.
2. Fold several pleats around the open end and staple them in place. Add more pleats if necessary to make the opening fit snugly around the forehead.
3. Cut a large face from construction paper. Cut features from scraps and glue onto face. Add details with markers. Glue the face onto the bag.
4. Add hair to puppet with markers or yarn.
5. Punch two holes in the bottom rim of the bag and add yarn ties.

USE:
Put the puppet on a child's head and tie the yarn ends together under the chin. Have the child kneel behind a table so that the audience sees only the puppet's head and the child's hands. The action of hands, head movements, and voice becomes a unique show.

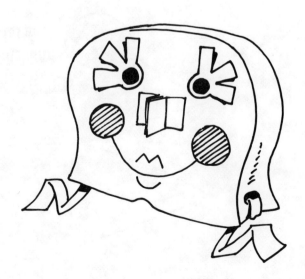

Trash Bag Puppet

Produce this puppet with only two common materials.

MATERIALS:
Paper plate
Stapler
Colored markers
Thin foam rubber strip
Medium-sized plastic trash bag
Scraps of felt, fabric, paper, buttons, etc.

CONSTRUCTION:
1. Fold the paper plate in half and crease it at the center.
2. Draw a mouth on the inside of the plate with markers.
3. Staple the foam rubber strip to the plate as illustrated.
4. Cut off the bottom part of the trash bag and discard. Staple one open end of the bag to the edge of the plate all around, turning under a 1″ seam as you go.
5. Form the facial features out of scraps and odds and ends. Glue eyes and eyebrows to the foam rubber strip.

USE:
Put hand through the trash bag drape and into the paper plate to work the mouth.

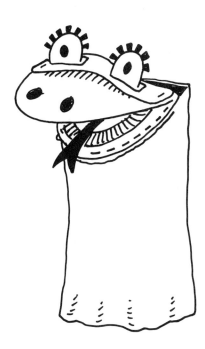

Foam Rubber Puppet

Foam rubber makes an almost lifelike animated puppet.

MATERIALS:
12″ square of foam rubber, ¼″ to ½″ thick
Scraps of felt, fabric, yarn, colored paper, buttons
Stapler
Rubber cement

CONSTRUCTION:
1. Staple two sides of the foam rubber together to form a tube.
2. Form the puppet's face by putting one hand in the tube and tucking the edges in to make a wide cuff. Thumb and fingers should be inside the cuff.
3. Bend wrist forward to form the head. Continue to shape the foam until satisfied with the look of the face.
4. Construct and glue on the facial features one by one, putting the puppet on the hand to guide their placement.

USE:
This puppet's face and mouth can be very expressive.
Experiment with the great variety of movements that thumb and fingers can make.

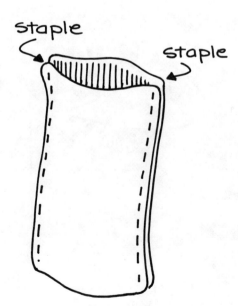

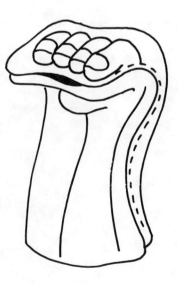

Tongue Depressor Puppet

Make the puppet and the mini puppet stage for a complete show.

MATERIALS:
Tongue depressor
Double-stick tape
Scraps of fabric, yarn, ric-rac, lace
Colored markers
Pipe cleaners (optional)

CONSTRUCTION:
1. Draw the face of the puppet on the tongue depressor.
2. Cut fabric for clothes and attach with double-stick tape. Add details, such as a belt, tie, or collar by gluing on yarn and ric-rac.
3. Draw hair with markers or glue on yarn hair.
4. Add arms with strips of fabric or pipe cleaners.

USE:
Make the puppet stage described on the following page to accompany these puppets.

Mini Puppet Stage

This stage is the perfect backdrop for tongue depressor puppets.

MATERIALS:
9″ x 12″ cardboard
Picture of scenery from a magazine or old calendar
Construction paper
Rubber cement
3½″ x 12″ posterboard

CONSTRUCTION:
1. Cut the picture to fit the cardboard.
2. Glue the picture onto the cardboard.
3. Fold the cardboard as illustrated, bending the side flaps forward.
4. Trim the edge of the cardboard with construction paper.
5. Bend the posterboard strip as illustrated. Glue the strip to each side flap.
6. Add props such as trees or a fence.

USE:
Hold the stage in one hand while manipulating the tongue depressor puppet with the other hand. Hold the puppet so that the top half of it can be seen by the audience. Try drawing a face on one finger to add to the show.

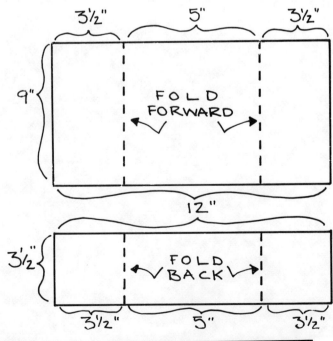

Pop-Up Puppet

Surprise the audience when this puppet comes out of hiding.

MATERIALS:
Nylon stocking (8″ length + extra hose fabric)
Cardboard thread cone or cone made of posterboard
Fabric
Dowel
Rubber band
Needle and thread
Scraps of cotton, yarn

CONSTRUCTION:
1. Stuff the toe of the stocking with extra hose fabric. Poke the dowel into the toe and secure with the rubber band.
2. Sew facial features in the stocking with needle and thread.
3. Insert the dowel into the large end of the thread cone. Stretch the rest of the stocking around the outside of the cone.
4. Poke holes in the narrow end of the cone. Sew the stocking to the cone end.
5. Add fabric arms, clothing, and yarn or cotton hair.

USE:
Hold the cone in one hand and use the other to move the puppet by means of the dowel. Make the puppet pop up from the cone and look around, then disappear again.

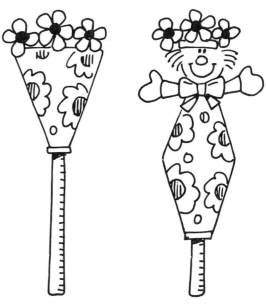

Body Puppet

Dance around the stage with this child-size puppet.

MATERIALS:
Large cardboard circle or rectangle
Four 4" x 48" strips of fabric
Large piece of fabric or wallpaper
36" length of yarn
Paper plate
4 rubber bands
Scraps of yarn, felt
Buttons
Colored markers
White glue

CONSTRUCTION:
1. Design the face of the puppet on the paper plate with colored markers, scraps, and buttons.
2. Glue on fabric or wallpaper to cover the large piece of cardboard.
3. Staple the paper plate to the cardboard.
4. Glue the fabric strips to the back of the cardboard as arms and legs.
5. Staple rubber bands to the ends of the arms and legs. Adjust the length of the fabric strips to the wearer, if necessary.
6. Punch a hole at each shoulder of the puppet. Cut the yarn in half and tie a length through each hole.

USE:
Tie the yarn around child's neck. Slip the rubber bands over wrists and ankles. The puppet will move with the child.

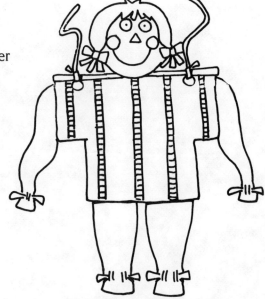

Caterpillar Rod Puppet

Make this puppet with honeycomb tissue from a craft supply store.

MATERIALS:
Green honeycomb tissue paper
Red, black construction paper scraps
White glue
2 craft sticks

CONSTRUCTION:
1. Cut the honeycomb tissue into a circle and pull it out to its full length.
2. Cut two eyes from the black paper and a mouth and tongue from the red. Glue features onto the front section of the tissue circle.
3. Dab a small amount of glue on the end of one craft stick and insert it into the tissue just behind the face. Repeat, gluing the other stick about halfway down the body. Compress the honeycomb tissue and allow to dry.

USE:
Hold a craft stick in each hand and move the caterpillar along a table top. The caterpillar can inch along or move from side to side, depending upon hand motions.

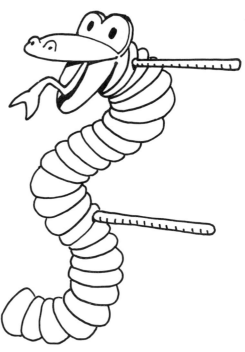

Jumping Jack Puppet

Add lots of motion to puppet plays with this puppet.

MATERIALS:
Tracing paper
Posterboard
4 brass paper fasteners
Scraps of colored paper, yarn, fabric
String
Plastic curtain ring (or any small ring)

CONSTRUCTION:
1. Trace the patterns on the next page and cut them out.
2. Outline the body, two arms, and two legs on the posterboard. Cut out all the parts. Punch holes where indicated.
3. Add clothing, hair, eyes, and other details with the scraps of paper, yarn, and fabric.
4. Fasten the arms and legs loosely to the body with the brass paper fasteners.
5. Cut an 18″ length of string. Thread it through the remaining holes as shown. Tie on the plastic ring as a handle.

USE:
Pull down on the ring at the back to operate the puppet. The puppet's arms and legs will fly up.

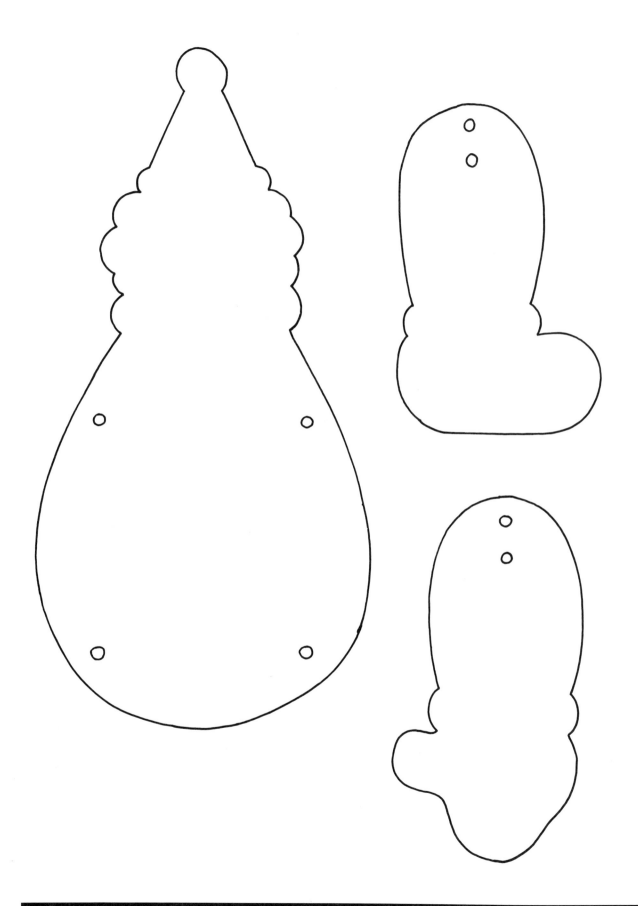

Mop Puppet

Make a furry creature from a fluffy dust mop.

MATERIALS:
Dust mop head
Scraps of yarn, felt, fabric, telephone wire
Buttons
White glue
Needle and thread

CONSTRUCTION:
1. Put one hand inside the mop. Arrange the strands where the face will be and cut off any excess strands.
2. Determine where the facial features should go. Cut eyes from felt or fabric and glue on. Add eyebrows, whiskers, a nose, ears, eyeglasses, or a hat. Glue or sew features in place.

USES:
A mop head makes a great dragon with a long red felt tongue. You can also create a lion, a bear, or a bearded old man.

Folded Puppet

Create dozens of clever designs with this simple construction.

MATERIALS:
Posterboard rectangle, any size
Colored markers
Stapler

CONSTRUCTION:
1. Fold the posterboard in half crosswise. Fold each half in half again toward the center crease.
2. Refold along the center crease.
3. Use scissors to make a single cut from the center crease to the outer creases, as illustrated. This cut is the mouth.
4. Open the posterboard and draw the face on the two middle panels with colored markers.
5. Form a triangular tube from the posterboard, overlapping the two outer panels. Staple at top and bottom.

USE:
Hold the back of the tube at the bottom to manipulate the puppet. Shake the puppet to make the mouth open and close.

Milk Carton Puppet

Make a whole family of milk carton people.

MATERIALS:
Quart or half-gallon milk carton
Self-adhesive paper
Utility knife
Odds and ends: paper, yarn, buttons, bottle caps, foil
White glue

CONSTRUCTION:
1. Fold in the top of the milk carton to square it up.
2. Cover the carton with self-adhesive paper.
3. Slit the carton across the middle on three sides with the utility knife. Fold back the halves along the fourth side. The opening becomes the puppet's mouth.
4. Create the features with odds and ends and glue on.

USE:
Put thumb and fingers in the two sections and move the mouth to make the puppet speak.

Maxi Puppet Stage

This stage is perfect for big puppets.

MATERIALS:
Large appliance box
Children's artwork
Yarn
2 large paper fasteners
Tempera paint

CONSTRUCTION:
1. Cut the flaps from the box. Cut three sides of a large square on the front of the box as show. Cut a child-size door in the back of the box.
2. Attach the yarn to the flap with a paper fastener. Place the second paper fastener in the top of the box so that the flap can be tied shut.
3. Paint the box with tempera paint, then decorate it with children's artwork. Students may also paint scenery on the box, or add scenery as described in "City Buildings" on the next page.

USES:
1. One or two students can perform inside this puppet stage. The back door allows for easy change of performers between scenes, as needed.
2. If desired, add a curtain to the puppet stage by threading two hemmed squares of fabric on a long piece of elastic. Attach the elastic ends inside the box on either side of the opening with sturdy thumbtacks.

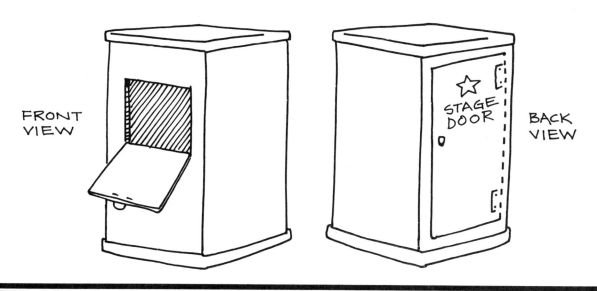

FRONT VIEW

STAGE DOOR

BACK VIEW

City Building

All puppeteers can help make stage sets for their puppet plays.

MATERIALS:
Cardboard base
Boxes of all shapes and sizes
Cardboard tubes
Variety of colored paper, cardboard, posterboard
Aluminum foil
Odds and ends: bottle caps, felt, 35 mm slides, stryofoam, straws, string, wire

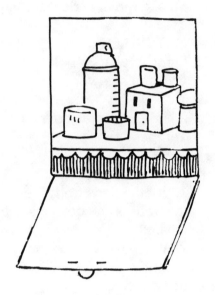

CONSTRUCTION:
1. Plan the position of buildings, parks, rivers, and streets on the cardboard base. Glue on green paper for a park, foil for streets, or materials to mark other areas.
2. Design the boxes as buildings with a variety of paper coverings. Use odds and ends to add doors, windows, and other small features. Place a flag on top of a post office or school.
3. Glue the buildings in place. Use odds and ends to add details such as lampposts, mailboxes, signs, trees, and telephone poles.

USES:
Puppet plays may call for a western setting, a space-age city, or a small town in rural America. Details such as a white picket fence, a horse trough, or a jail with bars will add to the performance by setting the tone of the play.

   City Building can also be used as a problem-solving activity. Challenge students to use limited materials to create an environment.

COSTUMES

Basic Pillowcase Costume

Create the costumes on the following pages from this pattern.

MATERIALS:
Pillowcase
Permanent markers
Thick yarn (optional)

CONSTRUCTION:
1. Put the hemmed opening at the top or bottom according to the directions for each costume.
2. Cut the neckline in one of these ways: a V-shaped cut, a round cut with a slit in the back, a U-shaped cut, or a square cut.
3. Add details with permanent markers or extra fabric which you staple on.
4. Create a gathered effect by cutting a slit in the hem and running a length of thick yarn through it. Tie the two ends together, puckering the hem at the neck, waist, or legs, as desired.

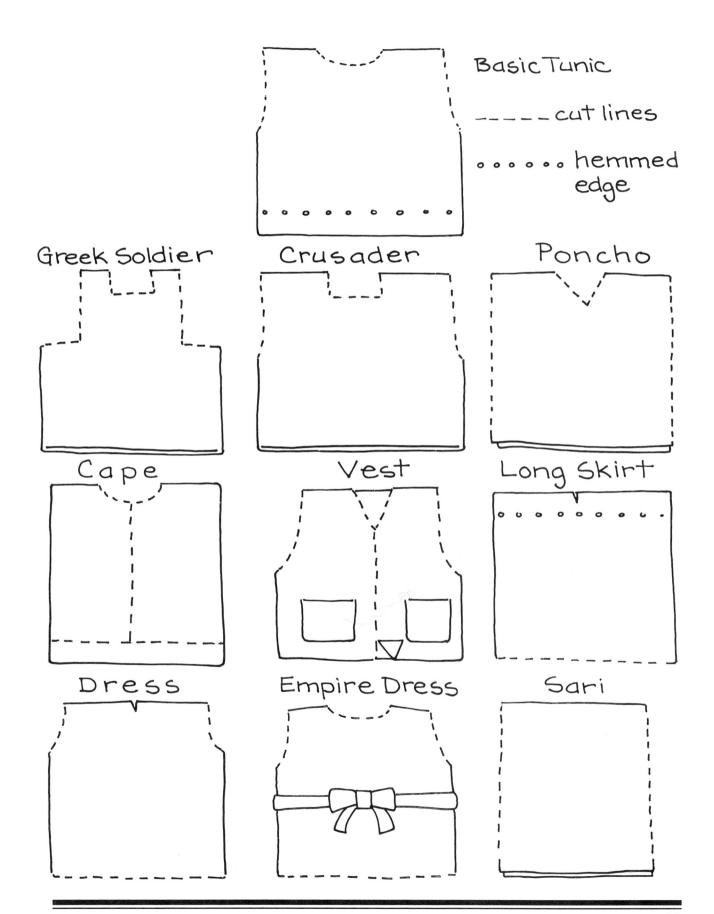

Basic Tunic

------ cut lines

o o o o o o hemmed edge

Greek Soldier

Crusader

Poncho

Cape

Vest

Long Skirt

Dress

Empire Dress

Sari

Clown

This costume features a drawstring at the neckline.

MATERIALS:
Pillowcase
Colorful felt scraps
Thick yarn
Paper plate
Colored markers
Hole punch

CONSTRUCTION:
1. Place the hemmed opening of the pillowcase at the top of the costume. Slit the hem and gather with yarn.
2. Cut armholes in the sides of the costume. Cut scalloped legholes at the bottom.
3. Cut colorful circles of felt and staple them all over the costume.
4. Cut eyes in the paper plate for eyes, nose, and mouth.
5. Outline the mouth and nose with red marker, the eyes with black. Add red cheeks and black tears under the eyes.
6. Punch a row of holes along the top of the mask. Tie short lengths of yarn through the holes, fraying the yarn to create the hair.
7. Punch a hole in each side of the mask and add yarn ties.

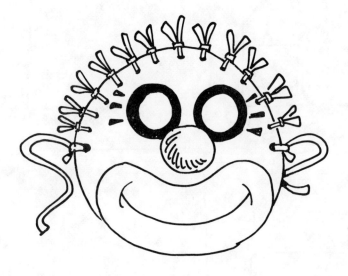

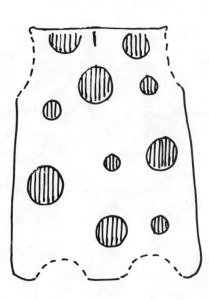

Flapper

Design a party dress right out of the 1920s.

MATERIALS:
Pillowcase
Chenille fringe (or any fringe found in fabric store)
Paper plate
Yarn (brown, black, red, or yellow)
Colored markers
Hole punch

CONSTRUCTION:
1. Place the seamed end of the pillowcase at the top of the costume. Cut a rounded neckline and two armholes.
2. Staple the fringe around the neck, armholes, hemline, and down the front of the dress.
3. Cut holes in the paper plate for eyes, nose, and mouth.
4. Draw eyebrows, eyelashes, and cheeks with colored markers.
5. Cut the yarn in 4–5″ lengths for the hair.
6. Punch holes close together along the top of the mask. Tie on the yarn through the holes.
7. Punch a hole in each side of the mask and add yarn ties.

Lizard

Make this reptile for an especially creepy effect.

MATERIALS:
Pillowcase
Green vinyl
Green crayon
Black permanent marker
Tracing paper
Mask patterns
Red felt
Green and black yarn
Stapler

CONSTRUCTION:
1. Place the seamed end of the pillowcase at the top of the costume. Cut a jagged neck opening and armholes, as shown.
2. Cut a small U-shaped opening in the center of the hemmed end to create legs.
3. Feed green yarn through the hem to form a drawstring for each leg.
4. Unwrap a green crayon and rub it on its side to color the costume.
5. Draw scales on the costume with black permanent marker.
6. Cut a tail from green vinyl and staple it to the costume.
7. Trace the mask patterns and cut them out.
8. Fold vinyl in half. Place mask pattern on fold line and outline it. Cut out mask and eyeholes.
9. Glue black yarn to mask to decorate eyes and form shapes around the mouth.
10. Outline tongue pattern on red felt and cut out. Staple in place.
11. Punch holes and add yarn ties to mask.

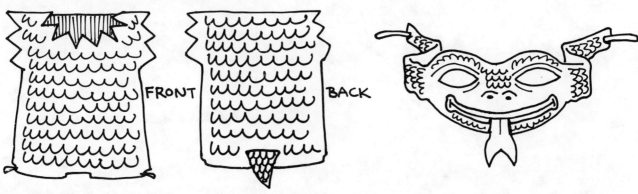

FRONT

BACK

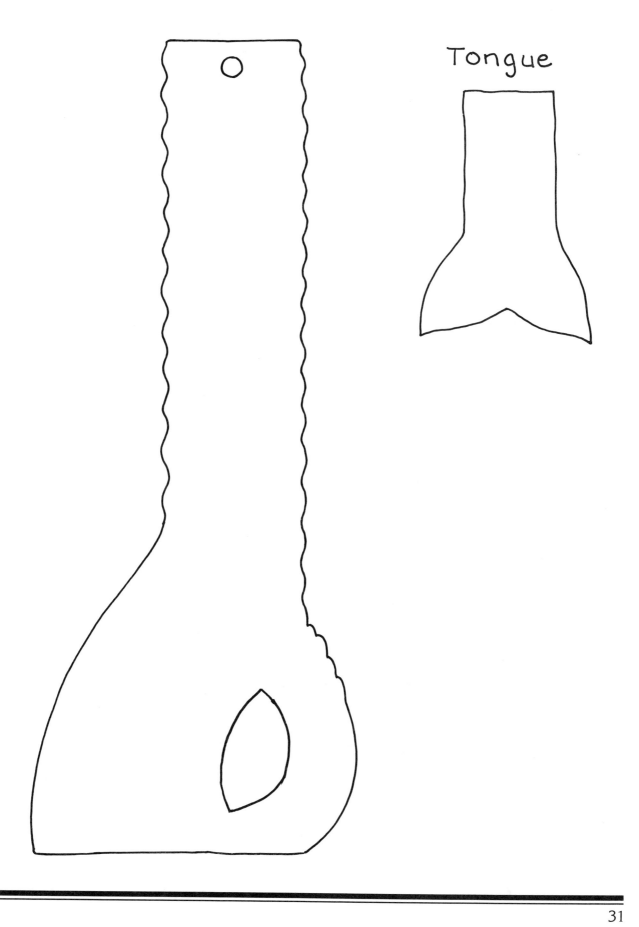

Tongue

Baseball Player

Make a favorite baseball player's uniform.

MATERIALS:
Pillowcase
3 black buttons
White glue or needle and thread
Permanent markers
Square box that fits the head
Construction paper

CONSTRUCTION:
1. Place the seamed end of the pillowcase at the top. Cut a V-shaped opening for the neck. Cut armholes.
2. Glue or sew the buttons down the front of the shirt.
3. Draw your favorite team's name, symbols, and numbers. (Examples: stripes for Yankees, a big R for Royals, a halo for Angels.)
4. Cut off three of the box flaps, leaving one for the bill of the hat.
5. Cover the box and the flap with construction paper in your team's colors.
6. Draw the team's initials, matching the uniform, on the front of the cap.

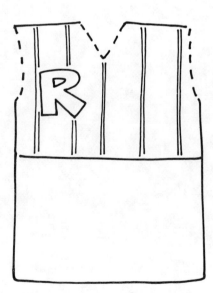

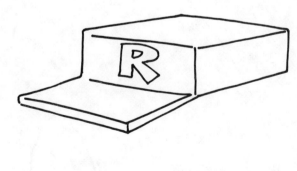

Coat and Tails

Make this version of the pillowcase costume for a formal party.

MATERIALS:
Pillowcase
Black felt
White glue
2 small black buttons
2 large black buttons
Needle and thread (optional)
Black posterboard
White ribbon

CONSTRUCTION:
1. Place the seamed end of the pillowcase at the top and cut a V-shaped neck opening. Cut two armholes.
2. Cut the vest in front and tails in back, as shown.
3. Cut a bow tie from black felt and glue it in place.
4. Glue or sew the two small buttons under the bow tie and the large buttons on the back, as shown.
5. To make the top hat, cut a rectangle from black posterboard that will fit around the head with a 2″ overlap.
6. Form a cylinder from the rectangle and staple to fasten.
7. Trace one end of the cylinder on black posterboard. Draw another circle 3″ outside the first one to form hat brim. Cut out.
8. Cut slits 2″ deep, about 1″ apart, at one end of the cylinder. Bend up these tabs.
9. Slip the brim over the cylinder. Glue or staple the cylinder to the brim.
10. Trim the hat with white ribbon.

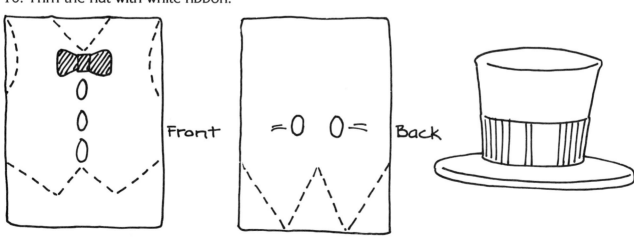

Front   Back

Basic Paper Costume

Create the costumes on the following pages with these directions.

MATERIALS:
12″ wide kraft paper, sturdy wrapping paper, or lightweight
 flexible plastic
Stapler
Yarn

CONSTRUCTION:
1. Cut four strips to the needed length. Place the strips in pairs.
2. Staple each pair together along half the length of one side, as shown. Open each pair.
3. Lay the pairs together and staple as shown, leaving room for armholes.
4. Punch rows of corresponding holes across the shoulders and down the front.
5. Lace yarn through the holes and tie to close the shoulders and front.

VARIATIONS:
1. To make a pullover top, shorten the strips and leave the bottom open.
2. Make a V-neckline by folding under the corners at the neck and stapling.

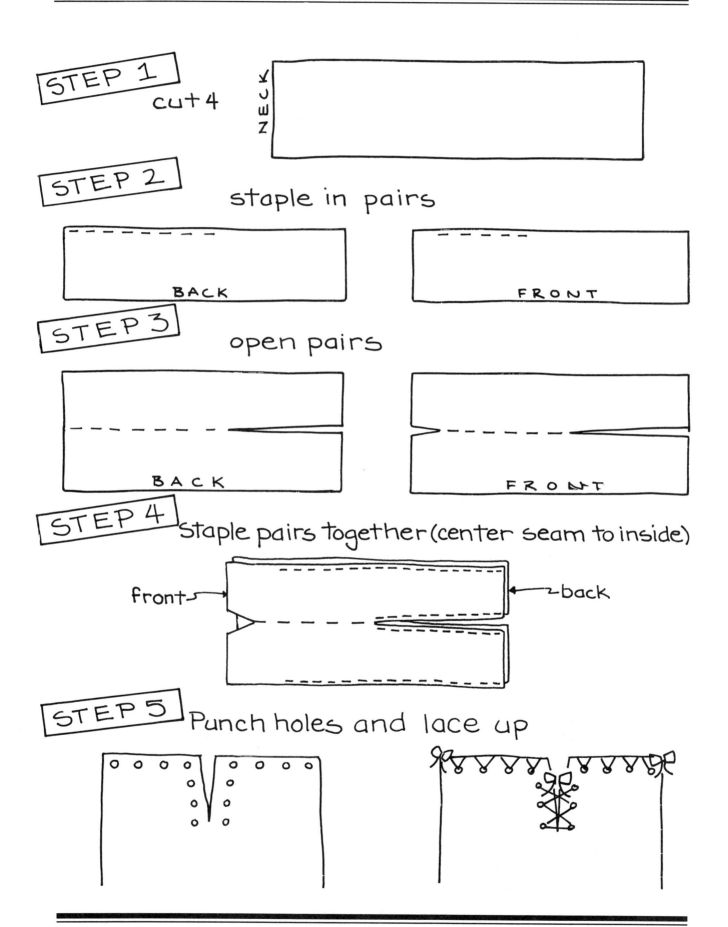

STEP 1 cut 4

NECK

STEP 2 staple in pairs

BACK

FRONT

STEP 3 open pairs

BACK

FRONT

STEP 4 Staple pairs together (center seam to inside)

front → ← back

STEP 5 Punch holes and lace up

Scarecrow

Lightweight plastic works well for this costume.

MATERIALS:
12″ wide lightweight plastic or paper
Yarn
Colorful construction paper scraps
Gold ribbon
White glue
Paper plate
Colored markers

CONSTRUCTION:
1. Make the basic costume described on page 34.
2. Cut lengths of gold ribbon and glue on at shoulders and ankles to look like straw.
3. Cut patches from construction paper and glue to costume.
4. Cut holes in paper plate for eyes, nose, and mouth.
5. Decorate the mask with yarn, construction paper, and markers.
6. Punch a hole in each side of the mask and add yarn ties.

Indian Shirt

Decorate this costume with Indian pictographs and fringe.

MATERIALS:
12″ wide brown wrapping paper
Yarn
Scraps of construction paper
2″ wide strips of paper in a contrasting color
White glue (optional)

CONSTRUCTION:
1. Follow the basic directions on page 34, using jacket-length strips. Make a V-neckline in the front and back.
2. Fringe the 2″ wide strips of paper along one side. Staple or glue fringe along the neckline, side seams, hem, and across the yoke as shown.
3. Cut Indian symbols from construction paper. (Examples: arrow, sun, paw print, canoe, feather.) Glue symbols to shirt.

Brown Bear

Follow these directions for any furry creature.

MATERIALS:
Brown kraft paper, 6–10' long x 30–36" wide
Glue or stapler

CONSTRUCTION:
1. Fold the paper in half crosswise.
2. Have the child lie on the kraft paper with shoulders at the fold line. Draw around the child as shown.
3. Cut away excess paper.
4. Cut a round neck opening, slitted in the back to fit over the child's head.
5. Glue or staple all edges as shown.
6. Cut narrow strips from the scrap paper for fur. Fringe the strips along one side and glue to the costume body in rows.

Fringe

Bee

Wear black clothing or leotard and tights beneath this costume.

MATERIALS:
2 sheets of oak tag, 27″ x 18″
Gold paper
White glue
8 strips of brown construction paper, 3″ x 18″
Thread cone or cone formed from posterboard
Eight 10″ lengths of gold yarn
4 sheets of yellow paper, 18″ x 9″
4 large paper fasteners
Telephone wire

CONSTRUCTION:
1. Cover one side of each sheet of oak tag with gold paper. Round off all corners with scissors.
2. Glue the strips of brown paper to the sheets of oak tag as illustrated.
3. Cover the cone with gold paper and attach it to the costume with telephone wire.
4. Punch a hole at each shoulder and on each side. Tie a length of yarn through each hole.
5. Cut four wing shapes from yellow paper at one time. Glue the wings together in pairs.
6. Fold back the flaps and punch two holes in each flap. Punch four holes in the back of the costume where the wings will go.
7. Attach the wings with brads.
8. Make the Insect Mask on page 58 to wear with this costume.

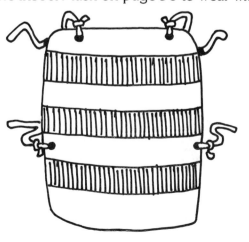

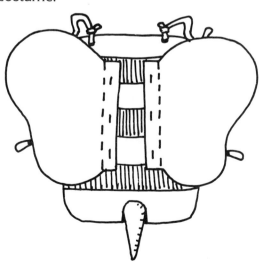

Knight in Armor

Wear this sandwich-board costume with a milk-jug helmet.

MATERIALS:
2 sheets of posterboard
Black or grey yarn
Silver paper or aluminum foil
White glue or rubber cement
Black permanent marker
One-gallon plastic milk jug
Scraps of foil, felt, ribbon, telephone wire, yarn, colored paper

CONSTRUCTION:
1. Cut the sheets of posterboard to the appropriate length and round off the corners.
2. Cut a round neckline, as shown.
3. Cut the paper or foil in strips or scallops. Glue on the armor to cover one side of each posterboard sheet.
4. Decorate the armor shapes with black permanent marker.
5. Punch a hole at each shoulder and two holes at each side. Tie a length of yarn through each hole to join halves of costume.
6. Cut out milk jug as shown on next page. The higher you cut, the larger the helmet will be.
7. Glue on various scraps to decorate the jug.
8. Add details with permanent marker.
9. Add a red scarf as a neck drape, a homemade shield, and sword to complete this costume, if desired.

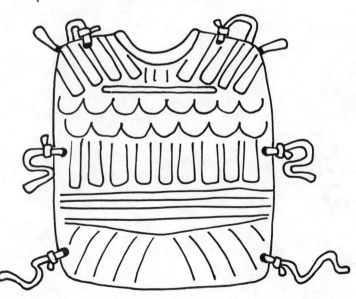

Lion

Make the king of beasts from a plastic trash bag.

MATERIALS:
Yellow 30-gallon trash bag
Masking tape
Yellow or gold yarn
Thick cord
Cardboard square, 10" x 10"
Tracing paper
Yellow or gold vinyl
Scraps of red vinyl or felt
White glue
Hole punch

CONSTRUCTION:
1. Cut a round neck opening in the bottom of the bag. Slit it in the back to fit over the head.
2. Slit open sides of bag. Make a cut under each arm as shown.
3. Overlap the side edges to form seams and fasten with masking tape on the inner side.
4. Wrap the heavy cord tightly with yarn and fasten ends with glue to make the tail.
5. Make a pompon by wrapping yarn around your hand several times. Tie all strands together tightly, then cut strands apart opposite the knot. Fray the ends, then fasten pompon to one end of tail.
6. Attach the tail to the back of the costume or to wearer's belt. (Cut a slit in costume if needed.)
7. Cut out a 6" circle in the middle of the cardboard square.
8. Trace the mask pattern and cut it out. Lay pattern on folded yellow vinyl and draw around it. Cut out mask.
9. Place mask inside the circle and staple the sides to the back of the cardboard.
10. Cut two ears from vinyl scraps and staple in place. Cut a mouth from red vinyl and glue onto mask.
11. Cover the cardboard with long lengths of yarn to form the mane. Staple or glue at one end and allow the rest to hang down. Staple or glue a row of yarn along the top of the mask to hang down at the back of the head.
12. Punch holes in the vinyl ends and add yarn ties.

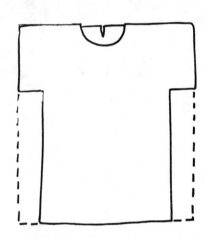

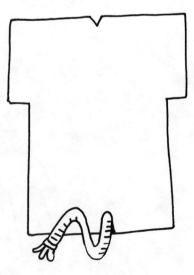

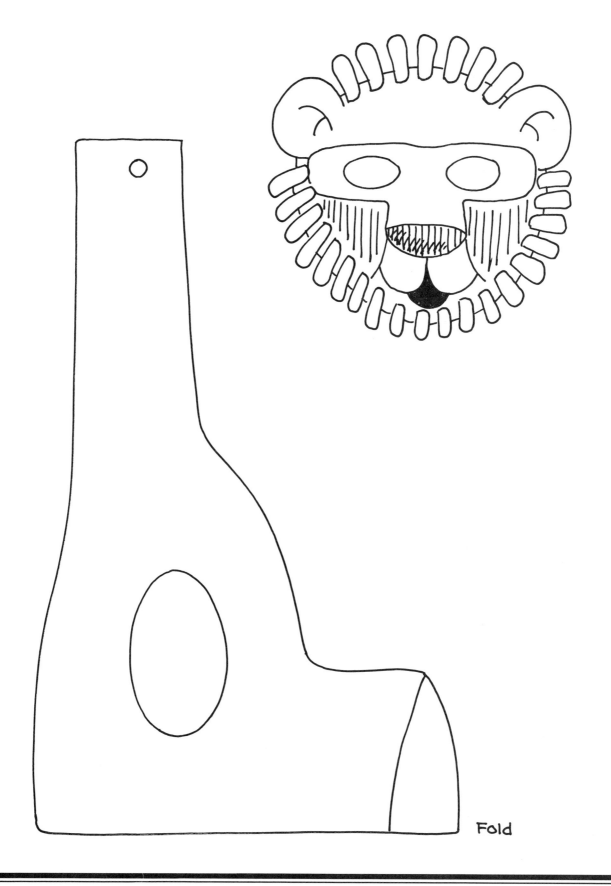

Fold

Fairy Princess

Transform trash bags into a special princess costume.

MATERIALS:
Two 30-gallon white trash bags
Masking tape
White paper or fabric
White yarn
Tracing paper
Silver or gold paper
White oak tag

CONSTRUCTION:
1. Cut a round neck opening in the bottom of one bag. Slit it in the back to fit over the head.
2. Slit open the sides of the bag and cut sleeves as shown.
3. Overlap the sides to form seams and tape on inner sides.
4. Cut a scalloped edge around the open end of the bag.
5. Cut a collar from white paper or fabric. Punch corresponding holes in the front yoke and lace with yarn.
6. Trace the star pattern and cut it out. Outline the pattern on silver or gold paper. Cut out enough stars to decorate dress and hat. Glue stars on dress and collar.
7. Form a cone to fit the head from oak tag. Staple together.
8. Glue remaining stars on cone.
9. Cut the second trash bag in half along the sides and bottom. Use one panel as the veil of the hat.
10. Stuff one end of the veil into the seam near the top of the cone. Secure with tape on the inside.
11. Punch a hole at each side of the hat and add yarn ties.

Bat

Turn a black trash bag into a scary bat costume for Halloween.

MATERIALS:
Black 30-gallon trash bag
6 cardboard strips, 2″ x 8″
Cardboard rectangle, 7″ x 9″
White posterboard scraps
White glue or rubber cement
Black yarn

CONSTRUCTION:
1. Slit open one side and the bottom of the trash bag.
2. Cut a V-shaped neck opening in the center of one long side. Scallop the edges of the bag as shown. Save the scraps.
3. Staple the cardboard strips to the wings.
4. Staple the sides together under each arm.
5. Cover the cardboard rectangle with the trash bag scraps.
6. Cut eye, nose, and mouth holes. Cut two fangs from white posterboard and glue them in place. Add black ears.
7. Punch a hole at each side of the mask and add yarn ties.

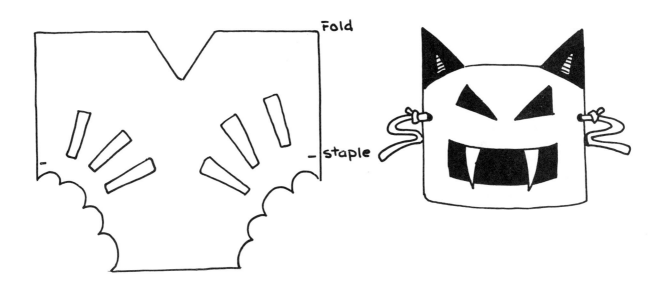

Basic Fabric Costume

Follow these steps to make several different costumes.

MATERIALS:
Fabric remnants
Stapler

CONSTRUCTION:
1. Fold a large piece of fabric in half.
2. Cut a hole in the center of the fold end for the head. Cut a 4″ slit in the back to allow room for easy removal.
3. Cut the sides to form the sleeves as shown. Adjust the size to fit the wearer. If the costume will be worn outside in cold weather, make it roomy enough to cover a heavy coat.
4. Seam the sides together with a stapler.

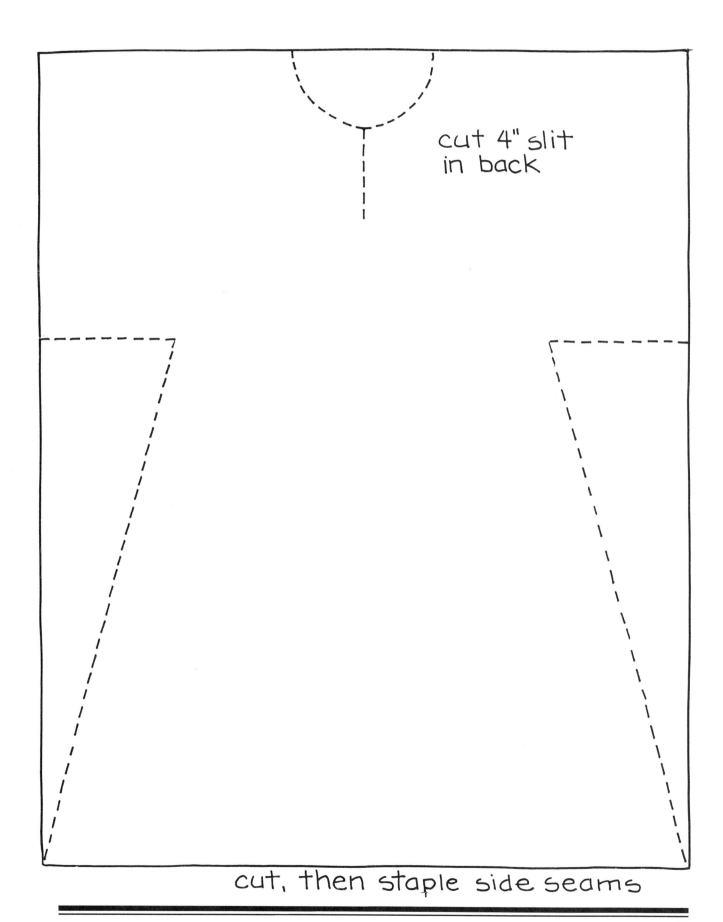

cut 4" slit
in back

cut, then staple side seams

Mouse

Create a furry friend with brown coat fabric or fake fur.

MATERIALS:
Brown fabric
4 or 5 rubber bands
2 cardboard circles, 5″ diameter
Paper plate
Utility knife
Thread cone
Glue
Telephone wire
Brown yarn

CONSTRUCTION:
1. Cut the fabric according to directions on page 46.
2. Staple the sides to fit.
3. Roll a strip of fabric into a long cylinder to form a tail. Secure it with rubber bands spaced along the length. Staple to costume.
4. Staple cardboard circles to paper plate to form mask.
5. Cut holes for eyes with a utility knife.
6. Cut a 2″ circle from the center of the plate for the nose. Poke the cone through the hole and glue it into place.
7. Add whiskers made from telephone wire.
8. Punch a hole in each side of the mask and add yarn ties.

Tail

Skunk

Here comes the smelliest animal in the forest!

MATERIALS:
Black fake fur
Large strips of white vinyl or paper
Black yarn

CONSTRUCTION:
1. Cut out the body of the skunk from fake fur according to the directions on page 46. (Since this is a very warm costume, there may be no need to allow room for a coat underneath.)
2. Cut a tail from fur and staple it to the back of the costume.
3. Cut out the hat and ears. Staple the ears onto the hat. Staple a yarn tie on each side of the hat.
4. Cut two large white strips for the body, a smaller strip for the tail, one for the hat, and two very small ones for the ears. Glue or staple all into place. (Cut the strips from reflective paper to allow better visibility at night.)

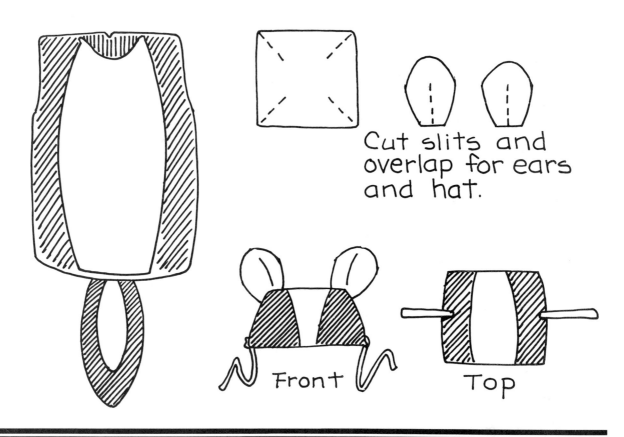

Cut slits and overlap for ears and hat.

Front   Top

Carrot

Adapt this walking, talking carrot to any other fruit or vegie.

MATERIALS:
Large piece of orange fabric
Paper plate
Stiff green ribbon
Orange yarn
Orange crayon or marker

CONSTRUCTION:
1. Cut out the costume from orange fabric according to the directions on page 46.
2. Cut holes in the paper plate for eyes, nose, and mouth.
3. Color the plate with orange crayon or marker.
4. Punch holes close together along the top of the plate. Loop lengths of green ribbon through each hole so that they stand up straight.
5. Punch a hole in each side of the paper plate and add yarn ties.

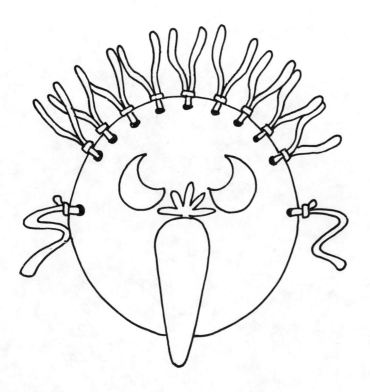

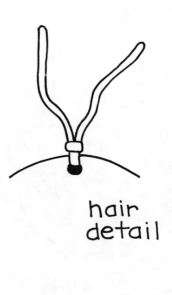

hair detail

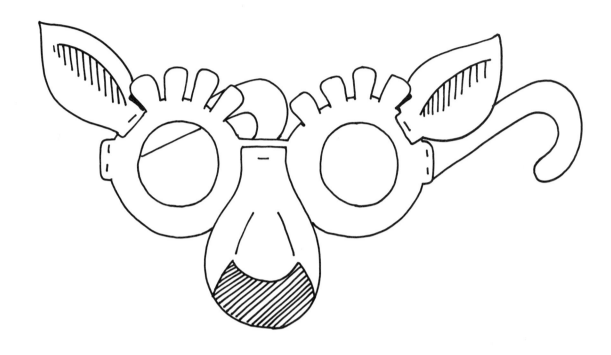

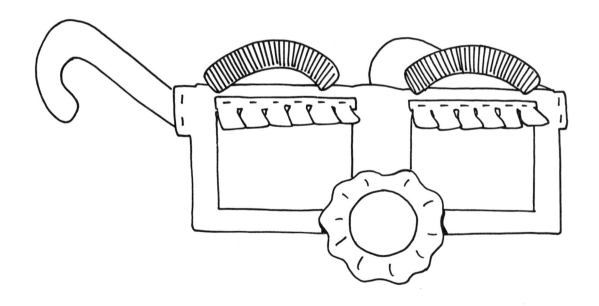

Primitive Mask

Create a variety of individual styles with this basic design.

MATERIALS:
Tracing paper
8½″ x 11″ cardboard or posterboard
Utility knife
Scraps of yarn, felt, fabric, twine, colored paper, feathers,
    telephone wire, lace
Crayons or colored markers

CONSTRUCTION:
1. Trace the pattern below and cut it out.
2. Draw around the pattern near the center of the cardboard or posterboard.
3. Cut out the opening for the eyes and nose with a utility knife.
4. Punch a hole at each side of the mask and add yarn ties.
5. Decorate the mask with odds and ends. Add color with crayons or markers if desired.

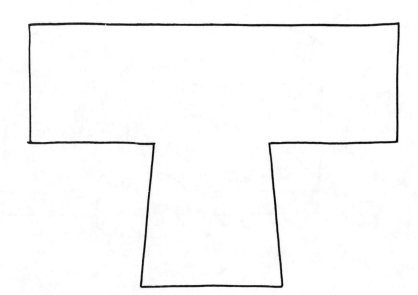

Funny Eyeglasses

Create props or entire masks with these glasses.

MATERIALS:
Two 35mm slide frames
Cardboard
Plastic six-pack holder
Glue
Odds and ends: egg cartons, felt, yarn, foam rubber, telephone
    wire, fruit trays, colored paper, vinyl, etc.

CONSTRUCTION:
1. To make 3-D glasses:
    a. Pop out the plastic film from the slide frames.
    b. Cut two earpieces and a nose bridge from cardboard.
    c. Glue or staple all of the pieces together.
    d. Add details such as eyelashes, nose, and eyebrows with
    odds and ends.
2. To make fancy glasses:
    a. Cut two adjoining rings from the six-pack holder.
    b. Cut two earpieces from cardboard and staple one at each
    side of the plastic rings.
    c. Add details like eyebrows, big ears, and a nose with the odds
    and ends.

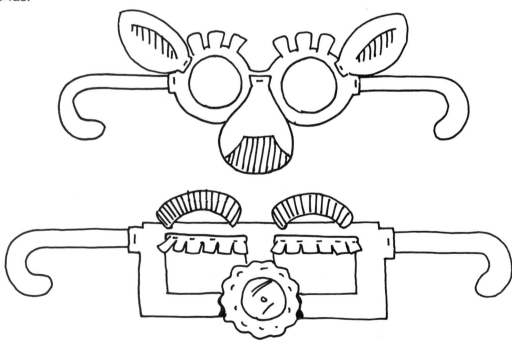

Vinyl Mask

One of these styles can accompany almost any costume.

MATERIALS:
Tracing paper
5″ x 20″ vinyl or other sturdy, flexible material
Yarn
White glue or rubber cement
Odds and ends: buttons, feathers, sequins, yarn, colored paper

CONSTRUCTION:
1. Trace the pattern of your choice and cut it out.
2. Fold the vinyl in half. Place the pattern on the fold line and draw around it.
3. Cut out the mask and the eyeholes.
4. Glue on the odds and ends to decorate the mask.
5. Punch a hole in each end of the mask and add yarn ties.

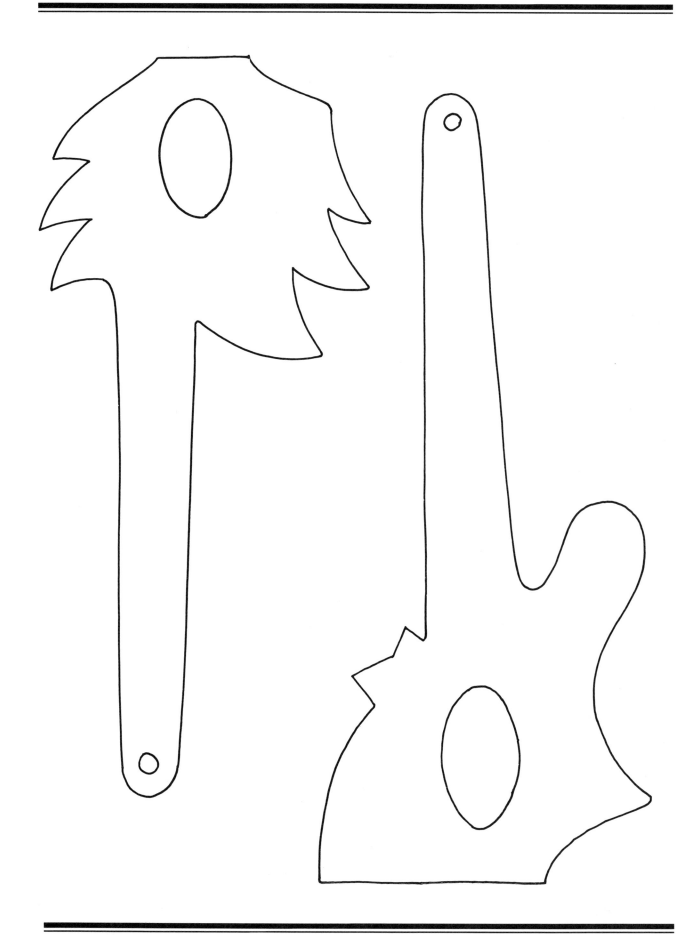

Visor Cap

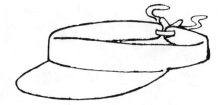

Make this cap at camp and wear it to the ballpark or beach.

MATERIALS:
Tracing paper
6″ x 9″ vinyl
20″ x 1½″ strip of vinyl
7″ x 9″ colored posterboard
6″ x 9″ oak tag
24″ length of yarn

CONSTRUCTION:
1. Trace the patterns on page 57 and cut them out.
2. Outline pattern #1 on colored posterboard and cut out.
3. Fold the colored posterboard over the center of the vinyl strip and staple it in place. Bend up the posterboard bill.
4. Cut slits in the posterboard as shown on pattern #1.
5. Outline pattern #2 on both the vinyl and the oak tag and cut out.
6. Bend the vinyl strip so that it is curved.
7. Glue the vinyl bill on top of the posterboard. Glue the oak tab bill on the bottom. Trim off the uneven edge.
8. Punch a hole in each end of the vinyl strip.
9. Cut yarn in half. Thread one length through each hole and knot.
10. Put the visor on and tie the yarn so that it fits comfortably.

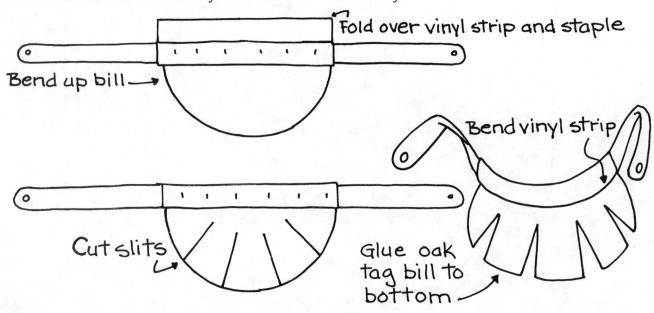

Fold over vinyl strip and staple

Bend up bill →

Bend vinyl strip

Cut slits

Glue oak tag bill to bottom →

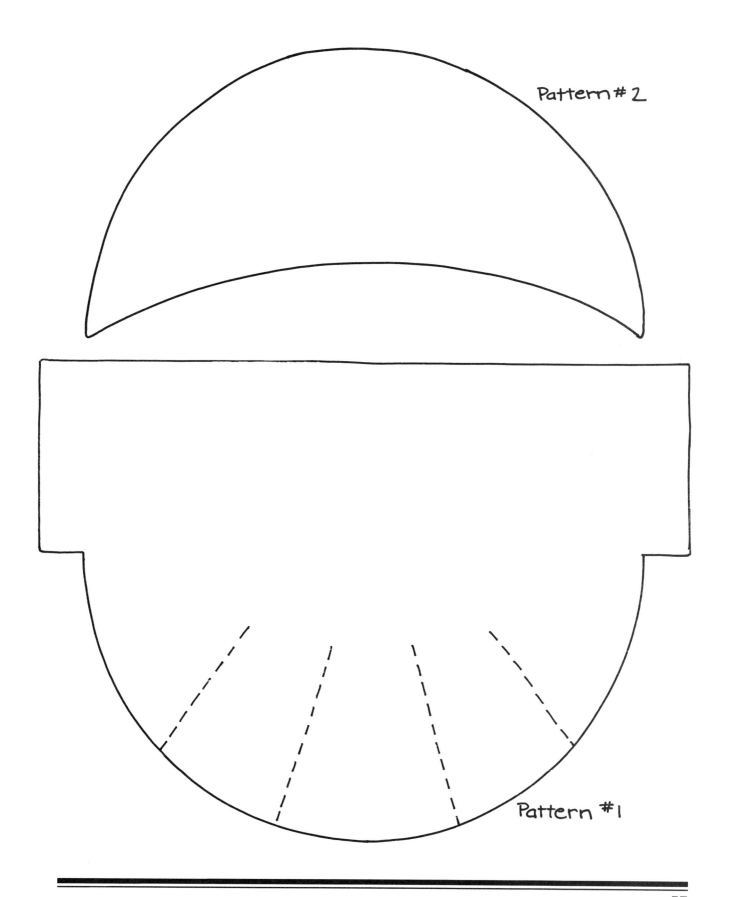

Pattern #2

Pattern #1

Insect Mask

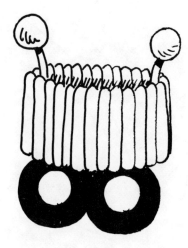

Wear this mask with the bee costume or any other bug suit.

MATERIALS:
3" x 25" strip of posterboard
Two 3" posterboard rings
Posterboard scraps or 2 drinking straws
Yellow or gold yarn
Black marker
Glue (optional)

CONSTRUCTION:
1. Form a headband from the posterboard and staple to fasten.
2. Color the posterboard rings black with the marker.
3. Wrap the entire headband with yarn, fastening the ends with glue or staples.
4. Staple on the rings for eyes.
5. Cut two antennae from posterboard or use drinking straws. Color them black and staple on above the eyes.

MUSICAL INSTRUMENTS

Pie Tin Tambourine

Start a kitchen band with this rhythm instrument.

MATERIALS:
Aluminum pie tin
Telephone wire or string
Bottle caps
Hammer
Nail
Self-adhesive paper (optional)

CONSTRUCTION:
1. Punch holes in the bottle caps with a hammer and nail.
2. Punch holes around the edge of the pie tin.
3. Attach each bottle cap with the wire or string.
4. Decorate the back of the tambourine with self-adhesive paper, if desired.

USE:
Hold the tambourine loosely in one hand. Shake it in time with the music. You can also clap your other hand to it while you are shaking it.

Rattler

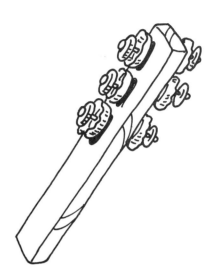

Make this instrument with a wooden stick or sturdy cardboard.

MATERIALS:
1″ x 2″ x 8″ wooden stick or tri-wall cardboard
Bottle caps
Spacers (wooden beads, buttons)
6 nails, 1½-2″ long
Hammer
Nail
White glue (optional)

CONSTRUCTION:
1. Punch a hole in each bottle cap with the hammer and nail.
2. Alternate bottle caps with spacers on each nail.
3. Hammer nails into one end of the stick or tri-wall cardboard. If you use tri-wall, dip the end of the nail in white glue before hammering.

USE:
Shake the rattler in time with the music. Make two of them and use them as maracas.

Finger Cymbals

Play these finger cymbals with folk dancing or singing.

MATERIALS:
2 bottle caps
Elastic thread
Hammer
Nail

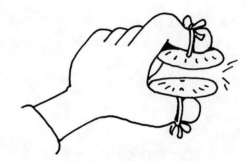

CONSTRUCTION:
1. Flatten the bottle caps with the hammer.
2. Punch two holes in each bottle cap with the hammer and nail.
3. Loop elastic thread through the holes and knot the ends together at the other side.

USE:
Hook fingers through the loops to clap the cymbals together.

Flatten bottle cap with a hammer.

Sand Blocks

Try different grades of sandpaper for different types of sounds.

MATERIALS:
2 thread spools
2 small, sturdy boxes
Sandpaper
Tape
White glue

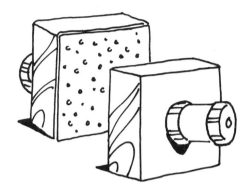

CONSTRUCTION:
1. Tape the box lids shut.
2. Cut the sandpaper to fit each lid.
3. Glue the sandpaper to the lids and let dry.
4. Glue a spool to the center of each box bottom and let dry.

USE:
Rub the sand blocks together in time to your favorite music. Try making different rhythms.

Bottle Chimes

Match the bottle tones to a piano scale.

MATERIALS:
8 glass bottles of the same size
Fork
Water

CONSTRUCTION:
1. Fill the bottles with different amounts of water.
2. Strike the bottles with the fork. Each will make a different tone.
3. Adjust the amount of water in each bottle so that you can play the notes of the scale.

USE:
Find the bottle that makes the highest note, then the one that makes the lowest note. Put the bottles in order and play the scale. Try to match the tones to notes on the piano. Then mark the water level on each bottle and write its musical note with a permanent marker.